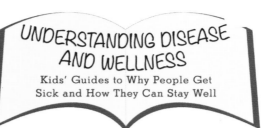

UNDERSTANDING DISEASE AND WELLNESS
Kids' Guides to Why People Get
Sick and How They Can Stay Well

A KID'S GUIDE TO
POLLUTION
AND HOW IT CAN
MAKE YOU SICK

VILLAGE EARTH PRESS

SERIES LIST

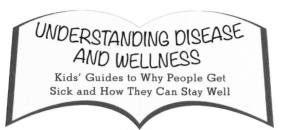

UNDERSTANDING DISEASE
AND WELLNESS
Kids' Guides to Why People Get
Sick and How They Can Stay Well

A KID'S GUIDE TO

POLLUTION

AND HOW IT CAN

MAKE YOU SICK

Rae Simons

Understanding Disease and Wellness:
Kids' Guides to Why People Get Sick and How They Can Stay Well
A KID'S GUIDE TO POLLUTION AND HOW IT CAN MAKE YOU SICK

Village Earth Press
Vestal, New York 13850
www.villageearthpress.com

First Printing
9 8 7 6 5 4 3 2 1

Series ISBN (paperback): 978-1-62524-445-1
ISBN (paperback): 978-1-62524-418-5
ebook ISBN: 978-1-62524-053-8

Library of Congress Control Number: 2013911245

Author: Simons, Rae

Note: This book is a revised and updated edition of *Pollution Can Make You Sick!* (ISBN: 978-1-934970-13-3), published in 2009 by Alpha House Publishing.

INTRODUCTION

According to a recent study reported in the Virginia Henderson International Nursing Library, kids worry about getting sick. They worry about AIDS and cancer, about allergies and the "super-germs" that resist medication. They know about these ills—but they don't always understand what causes them or how they can be prevented.

Unfortunately, most 9- to 11-year-olds, the study found, get their information about diseases like AIDS from friends and television; only 20 percent of the children interviewed based their understanding of illness on facts they had learned at school. Too often, kids believe urban legends, schoolyard folktales, and exaggerated movie plots. Oftentimes, misinformation like this only makes their worries worse. The January 2008 *Child Health News* reported that 55 percent of all children between 9 and 13 "worry almost all the time" about illness.

This series, **Understanding Disease and Wellness**, offers readers clear information on various illnesses and conditions, as well as the immunizations that can prevent many diseases. The books dispel the myths with clearly presented facts and colorful, accurate illustrations. Better yet, these books will help kids understand not only illness—but also what they can do to stay as healthy as possible.

—*Dr. Elise Berlan*

JUST THE FACTS

• There are three main kinds of pollution: air pollution, water pollution, and land pollution.

• Pollution can make people sick because pollution makes the Earth dirty, and people need the Earth—the air, the water, and the soil—to live.

• Pollution in the air, like smoke from burning coal or wood, can hurt your lungs, eyes, and throat.

• Air pollution can cause asthma, heart disease, and even cancer.

• Pollution in water can be dangerous when people drink water that is unclean or contains chemicals.

• Water pollution can make people sick, especially when industrial waste is dumped into the water people drink.

• Soil can become polluted when people bury waste, use chemicals to kill insects, or dump garbage into landfills.

• Global warming (also called climate change) does many bad things to the environment and human health. It causes air pollution, extreme weather, and human sickness.

• Taking care of the environment is important. Recycling, using cars less, and using less electricity are some ways to help take care of the Earth.

WHAT IS POLLUTION?

Pollution is what happens when we make our world dirty. Sometimes it's easy to see the dirt we've put into our environment—like when the sky over a city looks yellow and cloudy, or when water is green and smells bad. But other times, pollution is invisible. We may not be able to see the chemicals in the air, water, or land. But they are there. They can kill the Earth's plants and wildlife.

The three main kinds of pollution are:

- air pollution
- water pollution
- land pollution

Climate change (sometimes called global warming) is another problem that's also caused by pollution.

Although sometimes nature causes pollution—like when a flood washes dirt into a lake—the Earth can usually handle the pollution caused by natural events such as storms and floods. Most times, though, people cause pollution.

Factories like the ones in this picture put chemicals and tiny specks of dirt into the air and water. Cars, trucks, and airplanes make air pollution. Even our farms often put dangerous chemicals into the land and water. And then there's our garbage! So many human activities—from eating a candy bar to wrapping a birthday gift—make waste that has to be put somewhere. All this garbage usually ends up in landfills.

Pollution isn't bad just for the Earth, though. It's bad for people, too.

DID YOU KNOW?

Another kind of pollution is noise pollution. Too much noise can also hurt our environment. Noise can upset the balance of a natural *ecosystem*. This kind of pollution can hurt human health, too. It can damage our hearing. Being around loud noises—like the sound of machinery or jets—also adds stress to people's lives. Doctors have even found that high noise levels can raise people's blood pressure. This can make them seriously sick.

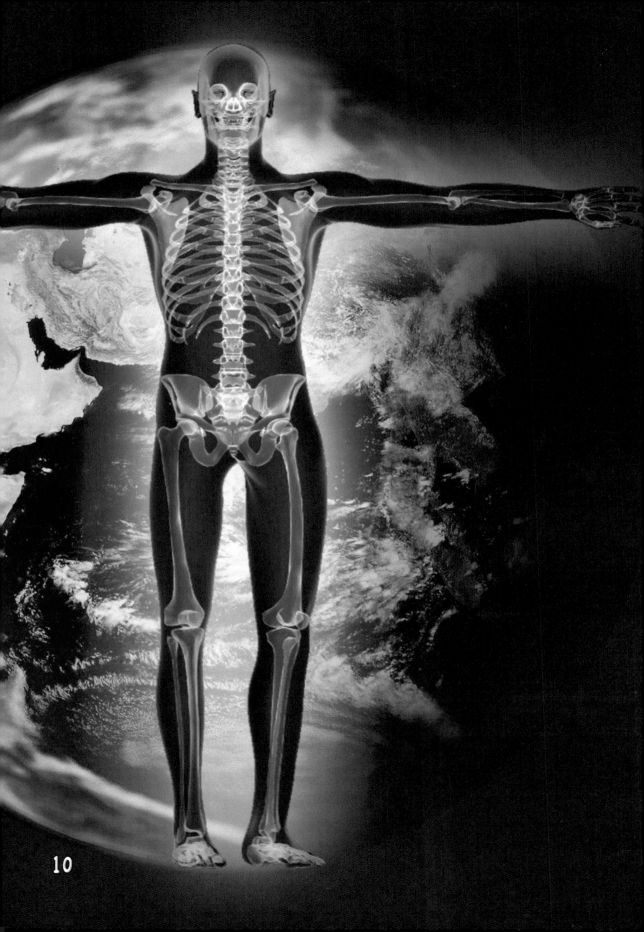

WHY DOES POLLUTION MAKE PEOPLE SICK?

Pollution makes people sick because all that dirt and garbage OUTSIDE ends up INSIDE our bodies.

Once upon a time, people thought of the Earth as though it were their mother. They loved Mother Earth and they respected her. They tried to understand her better. They knew that human beings need the Earth for food and water and air. They understood that if the Earth is sick, humans will be sick, too—and if the Earth dies, so will we!

Nowadays, many of us think that food comes from the store, already packaged in plastic or cardboard. We forget that everything we eat came from the land, from plants and animals. We think of water as something that comes out of the faucet whenever we want it. We forget that it comes from lakes and streams, from rainfall and snowfall, and from the sea. We *inhale* the air around us, and we don't think about what we're putting into our lungs.

WORDS TO KNOW

Inhale: to breathe in.

Pollution makes us sick because everything we eat, drink, breathe, and touch once came from the Earth. Because the outside world ends up inside our bodies, we need to keep Mother Earth healthy!

AIR POLLUTION

WHAT KINDS OF POLLUTION CAN MAKE YOU SICK?

DID YOU KNOW?

Every day, we breathe in and out about 20,000 liters of air. When that air is dirty, we are sucking in a lot of dust and chemicals!

LAND POLLUTION

12

WATER POLLUTION

CLIMATE CHANGE

AIR POLLUTION AND YOUR BODY

ASK THE DOCTOR

My family and I got stuck in a traffic jam inside a tunnel. The air smelled really bad and it gave me a headache. Am I going to get sick from breathing all that car exhaust?

A: Although constantly breathing polluted air can make you sick, most healthy people who breathe pollution like this for a short time will feel better as soon as they breathe clean air. If you notice any problems with your breathing, though, let an adult know. If the problem doesn't go away soon, you may need to see your doctor.

Air pollution can make your eyes, throat, and lungs sore. Your chest may feel tight or you may cough. Because exercise requires faster, deeper breathing, it may make these feelings worse. Some people are more bothered by pollution than others.

Air pollution can make you sick in different ways. And it's not just outdoor air that can harm you. Indoor air can also be polluted.

WHAT HAPPENS INSIDE YOUR BODY WHEN THERE'S POLLUTION OUTSIDE YOUR BODY?

Tiny specks from burning gasoline, coal, and wood can go deep into a person's lungs. From there, these tiny specks get into the bloodstream. When they do, they increase the chance of heart attack, lung cancer, and *stroke*. Air pollution acts like something scratching the inside of your lungs over and over. After a while, this can make you more likely to get some form of lung disease, such as *pneumonia*, asthma, or cancer.

WORDS TO KNOW

Stroke: bleeding in the brain, which can cause serious health problems, including death.

Pneumonia: an infection where the lungs become full of fluid.

15

ASTHMA

For most people, breathing is simple. They breathe air in through their noses or mouths, and the air goes into the windpipe (the trachea), down into the *bronchial tubes*, and from there into the lungs—and then back out again. But for people with asthma, breathing can be a problem. During an asthma attack, the bronchial tubes become swollen. Sometimes the lungs fill up with sticky *mucus*. When this happens, taking in a breath and letting it out is harder.

People with asthma need to take special medicine. Not being able to breathe can feel pretty scary.

An asthma attack is usually caused by a "trigger." It could be a change in air temperature or it could be an emotion, like when you get really angry. A lot of the time, though, triggers are something in the air, like pollen from plants, hair from a pet—or pollution. The two kinds of air pollution that are most likely to trigger an asthma attack are *ozone* (found in smog) and particle pollution (found in smoke and dust).

ASK THE DOCTOR

If I have asthma, does that mean I can't play sports?
A: No, it doesn't mean that at all. In fact, exercise can actually help your lungs work better—and many athletes have asthma. But because you have asthma, you need to be sure you take the medicines your doctor says you need, especially while exercising. (Make sure you tell your doctor you want to play sports.) And when the air quality is bad (for instance, on a hot day when the air is unusually smoggy), you may want to stay indoors or avoid exercising until smog levels go down. Exercise makes you suck more air into your lungs—and you don't want more ozone in there!

Asthma used to be rare, but now it is becoming more common than it ever was before. Doctors suspect that this is because of air pollution. Not only does air pollution trigger asthma attacks, but it makes you more likely to get asthma in the first place.

Children are especially likely to get asthma. In North America, asthma is now one of the most common illnesses in children; one child in every fifteen has it. This means that if you were in a class with fifteen students, at least one of you would probably have asthma. Why do so many children get asthma? It may be partly because they are more likely than adults are to be outside, running around.

People who have asthma will always have asthma. It's not a disease you outgrow—but that doesn't mean if you have asthma that you will always feel sick. Asthma medicines help keep the bronchial tubes from becoming narrow. Learning what triggers asthma attacks and staying away from those situations can also help a person with asthma not feel sick.

One of the best ways to prevent asthma, though, may be to clean up our air!

HEART DISEASE

The very small specks in dust, soot, and smoke can hurt your heart. When you breathe in these tiny pieces of dirt, they pass from your lungs into your blood, and from there they travel to other parts of your body, including your heart.

WORDS TO KNOW

Heart disease: sicknesses that keep your heart from working the way it should, including hardening of the arteries within the heart; heart failure, when the heart cannot pump blood normally; and arrhythmias, changes in the heartbeat.

Scientists have found that this is especially dangerous when it's combined with a high-fat diet. People in many developed countries are at danger, because many of them breathe in lots of air pollution AND they eat foods that are high in fat. The air pollution and the fatty diet combine to make blood vessels narrower and clogged. This can lead to *heart disease*.

Air pollution is especially dangerous for people who already have heart disease. Doctors say that people with heart conditions should stay away from places where air pollution is high. All of us should avoid exercising in areas where the air is more likely to be full of pollution. Instead of jogging or bicycling along busy streets, for example, go to a park to exercise. Find ways to exercise indoors when air pollution levels are especially high.

DID YOU KNOW?

Heart disease kills more than 7 million people each year. In North America, for example, it is the leading cause of death for both men and women.

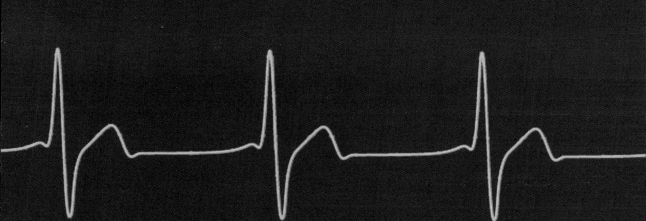

CANCER

Cancer is a disease where cells grow too fast. When this happens, the cells may eventually form tumors, growths that can invade normal body parts and keep other organs from working the way they should.

Chemicals found in air pollution **OUTSIDE** can trigger the abnormal cell growth that causes cancer **INSIDE**. According to the U.S. Environmental Protection Agency, more than 175 million pounds of cancer-causing chemicals are put in the air by factories each year. (And scientists say that number is just a little piece of the whole story, because it doesn't include the air pollution from cars and trucks, airports, power plants, incinerators, and other smaller polluters.)

Children are especially in danger from the chemicals found in air pollution. The *toxic* chemicals in pollution can cause *leukemia*, as well as other kinds of childhood cancers.

But it's not just the chemicals in air pollution that cause cancer.

WORDS TO KNOW

Toxic: poisonous, harmful to life.

Leukemia: a kind of cancer that makes the body produce too many white blood cells.

The small particles (the tiny, tiny specks) found in pollution can also cause this deadly disease. This kind of pollution is especially likely to trigger lung cancer, which is the leading cause of deaths from cancer in many countries. Over a million people die of lung cancer every year around the world.

When you inhale smoke, the tiny pieces of soot and dirt hurt the lining of your lungs. At first, your body will repair this damage, but after enough time goes by, your body may not be able to keep up with the repair work. This is when cancer can begin inside the lungs. Eventually, the cancer can travel from the lungs to other parts of the body. Doctors say that a person who breathes polluted air for long periods of time is as likely to get lung cancer as a person is who lives with a cigarette smoker.

ASK THE DOCTOR

If I live in a city with lots of air pollution, am I going to get cancer?

A: No! Not everyone who breathes air pollution gets cancer. But your chances are greater than if you lived somewhere with cleaner air. However, there are things you can do to help protect your body against cancer, even if you have to breathe air pollution every day, Eating plenty of fruits and vegetables is one of the best things you can do. These foods contain vitamins and other chemicals that help the body fight cancer.

WATER POLLUTION AND YOU

Water pollution happens any time dirt or chemicals get into water, making it unfit for natural and human uses.

WHAT DOES WATER POLLUTION LOOK LIKE ON THE **OUTSIDE?**

Water that is polluted may look brown or green. Clean water will be clear. You may see a film on top of polluted water. Sometimes you may not be able to see certain kinds of chemicals in water. If water is clean, though, wildlife, including fish, salamanders, frogs, and many kinds of insects, will live there. Polluted water will have only a few kinds of creatures (if any) living in it. All ecosystems need to be balanced—and pollution can throw off this *balance*. For example, too many chemicals of a certain kind can make plants and algae grow too fast and thick in the water. This in turn puts chemicals in the water that are bad for fish and other animals.

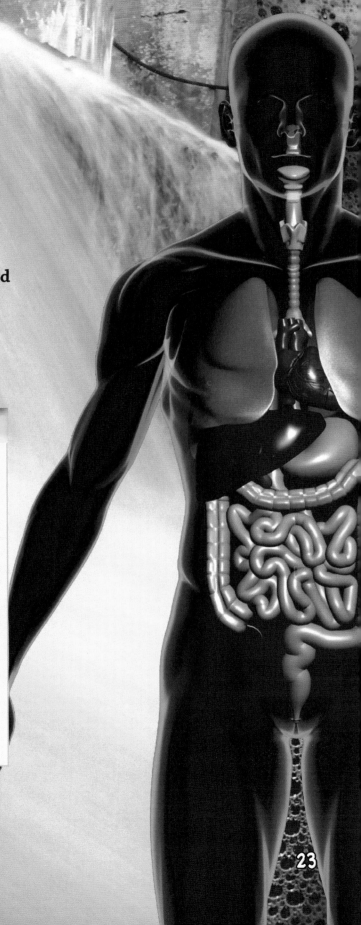

WHAT DOES WATER POLLUTION DO ON THE INSIDE OF YOUR BODY?

Your body needs water every day. If the water you drink contains pollution, germs and chemicals will enter your body. When they do, they can make you sick.

ASK THE DOCTOR

If my family drinks city water, it won't be polluted, right?

A: Probably not. Most cities in the United States, Canada, Australia, and Europe test their water carefully to make sure it is healthy. But the water you drink can also be polluted after it enters your house. Lead and copper from the pipes can get into drinking water. This is very bad for you. Find out what kind of plumbing your home has. If the pipes are lead or copper, only use cold water for drinking and cooking. Let it run for a while before you use it.

ASK THE DOCTOR

After my friends and I went swimming last week, we all got sick to our stomachs. How come?

A: You and your friends probably swam in water that had bacteria or viruses in it. This happens when sewage from bathrooms gets into the water. It can also happen if someone goes to the bathroom in the water. Most of the time, these illnesses aren't serious. You should see a doctor if this happens again, or if you don't feel better after a day or two.

WATER-BORNE DISEASES

Sometimes sewage from homes and farms leaks into the water supply. In some parts of the world, people dump human and animal wastes into streams and lakes that are also used for bathing and drinking. When this happens, germs from the **OUTSIDE** can get **INSIDE** your body. Sometimes tiny one-celled animals like the ones shown in the picture to the right live in water that's polluted. These little creatures can also make people sick.

Drinking or swimming in dirty water can give you a stomachache and diarrhea. It can make you throw up. Certain kinds of germs could also give you an itchy skin rash or a fever. Most of the time, these illnesses will make you feel uncomfortable, but you'll feel better soon. Other times, though, especially in parts of the world like Africa, Asia, and Latin America, polluted water can make you very, very sick. That's why it's a good idea to only drink bottled water if you live or travel in these areas of the world.

OUTSIDE

When factories and power plants do their jobs, they often make waste products. Many times this waste ends up in streams, lakes, and oceans. This kind of pollution is sometimes solid material, like sand. It could also be heat, which can upset the balance of the ecosystem by killing fish or making too many plants grow. Oftentimes, industrial wastes are various kinds of chemicals.

One of the worst kinds of chemical pollution is *mercury*. Mercury usually comes from power plants (where electricity is made) and waste incinerators (where garbage is burned).

WORDS TO KNOW

Mercury: a shiny, silvery metal that is very poisonous.

The mercury goes into the air, but then it falls to the ground. When it rains, the water washes over the ground and carries the mercury into streams and rivers. It gets inside fish—and it can get inside you if you eat that fish.

INSIDE

If even very small amounts of mercury get inside you, it can hurt your kidneys, liver, and brain. Your body cannot get rid of mercury by itself. This means mercury will gradually build up inside you. If it is not treated by a doctor, mercury poisoning causes pain, weakness, and loss of vision. Eventually, a person with mercury poisoning will not be able to move his muscles. He may even die.

DID YOU KNOW?

The Industrial Revolution was when machines and factories began to do people's work. This took place in the 1700s. It was when mercury pollution began.

Scientists believe that, on average, there is three times more mercury being washed into the Earth's water today than there was before the Industrial Revolution.

INDUSTRIAL WASTES

Industries also dump other kinds of pollution into waterways. Sometimes, for example, *petroleum* gets in the water accidentally, like when a tanker ship carrying oil crashes and spills its load into the ocean. Other times, petroleum gets into the ocean from off-shore oil drilling. Oil spills like this are very dangerous to the wildlife that lives in and on the water. Even years later, sea creatures may still be sick from the petroleum pollution.

People can also get sick when they eat fish and shellfish that have lived in water with this kind of pollution. When fish and other creatures die from petroleum pollution, their bodies decay and release germs. When this gets into the water humans use, people can also get sick.

WORDS TO KNOW

Petroleum: the oil that is pumped from within the Earth and used to make gasoline.

29

RADIOACTIVE POLLUTION

Radioactive pollution comes from nuclear power plants and nuclear weapons. However, hospitals and factories also put radioactive pollution into the Earth's waterways. These waste products are very dangerous to nature—and to humans.

Things that are radioactive can damage the *DNA* in animals and humans. This can cause babies to be born with something wrong with them. Radioactive pollution can also cause cancer.

OUTSIDE

Radioactive waste usually has no taste or smell. It is invisible. But it can be deadly to life on our planet. What's more, it doesn't go away quickly—some kinds of radioactive waste linger in the environmnent for as long as six hundred years.

INSIDE

Radioactive waste can make cells grow in strange ways. It gets inside your bones and causes bone cancer. It can damage the growth of *fetuses* inside their mothers.

WORDS TO KNOW

Radioactive: giving off harmful energy from the atoms inside a substance.

DNA: the material found within cells that passes along genes from parents to their children.

Fetuses: developing humans inside their mothers before they are born.

ASK THE DOCTOR

I've heard people say that nuclear power plants produce "clean" energy. Is that true?
A: Although nuclear power plants don't produce the kind of pollution that coal and oil do, waste from these plants can cause leukemia, thyroid cancer, bone cancer, and other forms of cancer. If an accident happens at a nuclear power plant, the danger to human life would be huge. Because of this, nuclear power plants should not be considered a safe answer to our energy problems.

WHEN YOUR HOME IS POLLUTED

DID YOU KNOW?

In 2006, in the United States alone, human beings produced 250 million tons of garbage. That's 4.6 pounds of garbage per person every day!

Your home could be your house, but it could also be the land where you live. And both can be polluted.

Household garbage, building materials, farm products, waste from mines, *fertilizers*, and *pesticides* can all make our homes polluted. These things are all dangerous to human life. Your home could make you sick!

WORDS TO KNOW

Fertilizers: chemicals and other substances added to soil to make crops grow better.

Pesticides: chemicals used to kill pests, whether plant or animal.

DANGER
Do Not Enter
Asbestos Contaminated
Area

For Information Call City Property

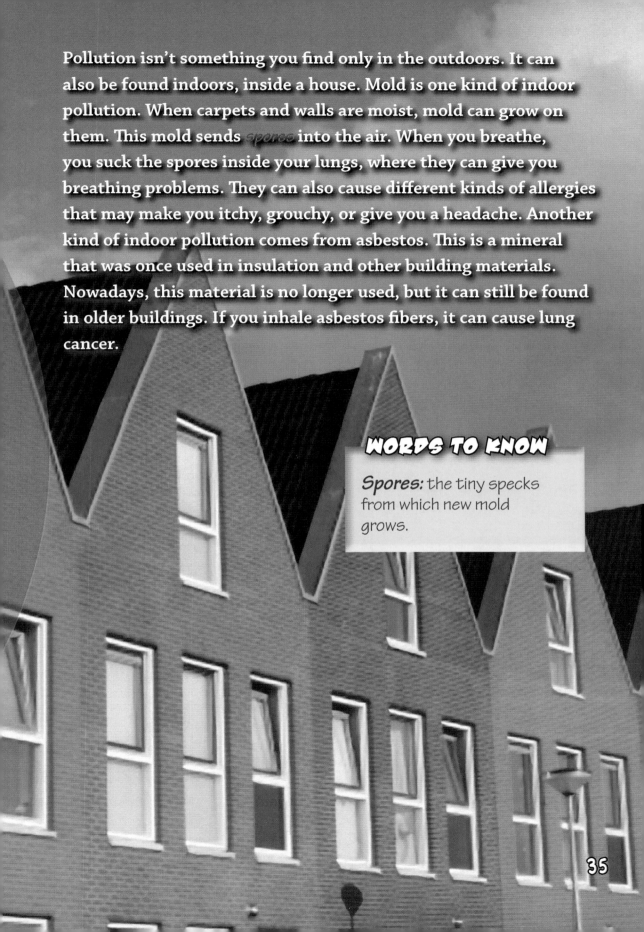

Pollution isn't something you find only in the outdoors. It can also be found indoors, inside a house. Mold is one kind of indoor pollution. When carpets and walls are moist, mold can grow on them. This mold sends *spores* into the air. When you breathe, you suck the spores inside your lungs, where they can give you breathing problems. They can also cause different kinds of allergies that may make you itchy, grouchy, or give you a headache. Another kind of indoor pollution comes from asbestos. This is a mineral that was once used in insulation and other building materials. Nowadays, this material is no longer used, but it can still be found in older buildings. If you inhale asbestos fibers, it can cause lung cancer.

WORDS TO KNOW

Spores: the tiny specks from which new mold grows.

POLLUTED SOIL

The Earth's soil can become polluted from several different sources. Here are a few of the ways:

• Buried waste containers can break.

• Pesticides and fertilizers can get into the soil from farms.

• Water that runs through *landfills* and garbage dumps can carry pollution into soil.

• Factories dump chemicals and other waste products directly into the ground.

• Acid rain carries chemical pollution in the air to the earth.

WORDS TO KNOW

Landfills: places where trash and garbage are buried beneath layers of dirt.

Soil pollution can be dangerous to people, especially children who often play in parks and playgrounds where they touch dirt. Some chemicals found in soil pollution cause cancers. Others, such as lead, can damage kidneys. Lead poisoning can also hurt children's brains and keep them from developing normally.

7283-3

THIS AREA CHEMICALLY TREATE KEEP CHILDREN & PETS OFF UNTIL DRY

WHAT DO WE DO WITH OUR GARBAGE?

DID YOU KNOW?

Wherever garbage ends up, it pollutes the Earth. Rainwater *leaches* through dumps and landfills, carrying germs and chemicals into the soil and waterways. When garbage is burned, the chemicals are released into the air instead, causing air pollution. The only good answer is to produce less garbage!

Finding a place to put our garbage is a big problem. In the days before plastic, the problem wasn't as serious. Paper, wood, and leftover food products eventually break down and go back into the soil. Plastic is a different thing altogether—it NEVER breaks down. That plastic candy wrapper you threw into the garbage today will still be around a hundred years from now, unless it's burned (which releases toxic chemicals into the air). In fact, it will still be around a thousand years from now!

When you throw something in a wastebasket, you probably never give it another thought. But think about all the millions of people in the world, all producing garbage of one sort or another every day. Where does all that garbage go?

Sometimes it goes to dumps, like the one shown in this picture. Sometimes it goes into landfills. Sometimes it goes into the oceans. Other times it gets burned in incinerators. Once in a while, it goes on a flat boat and floats around the world, looking for someplace willing to take it!

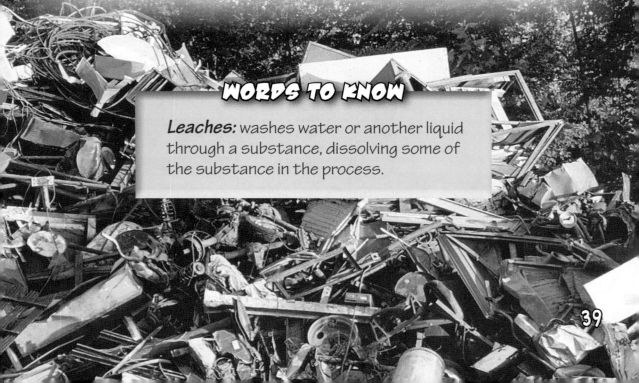

WORDS TO KNOW

Leaches: washes water or another liquid through a substance, dissolving some of the substance in the process.

GLOBAL WARMING AND YOUR BODY

ASK THE DOCTOR

My mom says that growing plants make us healthier. Is that true?

A: Your mother is right. Plants take in carbon dioxide and give off oxygen. That's the opposite from us: we breathe in oxygen and breathe out carbon dioxide. So plants and animals are the perfect balance for each other on our planet. Destroying acres of forests makes our planet less healthy. But keeping plenty of plants in your house can actually make the air you breathe healthier.

OUTSIDE YOUR BODY

Global warming is caused by the buildup of "greenhouse gases"—mostly *carbon dioxide*—in the atmosphere. These gases form a sort of blanket over the Earth, trapping in heat that would normally escape the atmosphere. When coal, oil, and gas are burned in our factories, vehicles, and homes, carbon dioxide goes into the air. This change in the Earth's atmosphere is also changing the Earth's climates.

WORDS TO KNOW

Carbon dioxide: a colorless gas that green plants use to create food.

40

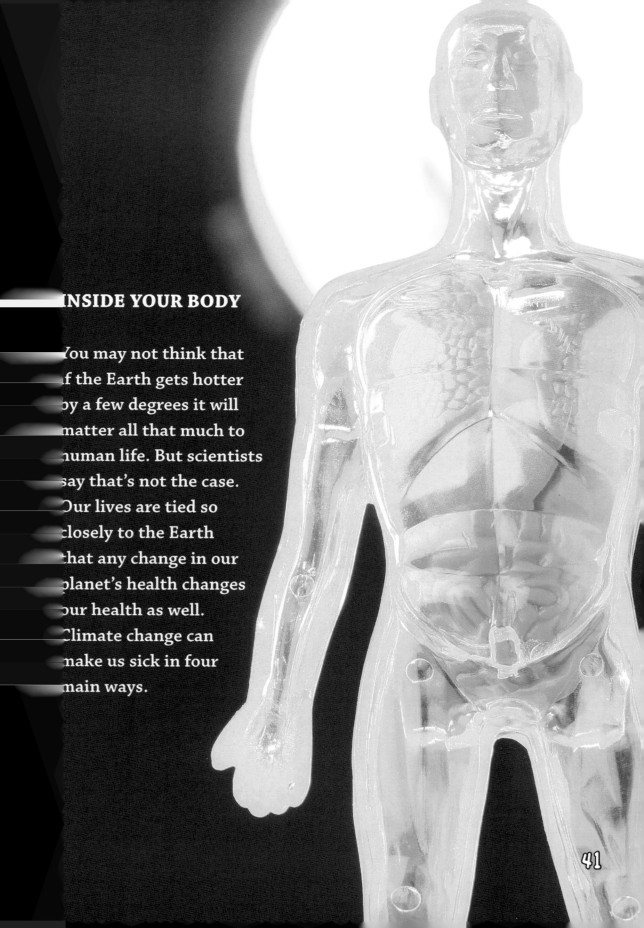

INSIDE YOUR BODY

You may not think that
if the Earth gets hotter
by a few degrees it will
matter all that much to
human life. But scientists
say that's not the case.
Our lives are tied so
closely to the Earth
that any change in our
planet's health changes
our health as well.
Climate change can
make us sick in four
main ways.

One of the first ways that global warming is making people sick is one you might not think about. But as temperatures get higher, there will be more of certain kinds of insects. Frost and cold temperatures normally kill the *larvae* of flies, mosquitoes, and fleas. But as the climate changes, nature's way to control insects will be destroyed. This means that there will be more mosquitoes, flies, and other insects in certain parts of the world.

ASK THE DOCTOR

My mother always says that flies are dirty and that they spread disease. Is that true?

A: Yes, it's true. Because flies crawl on and eat dead flesh and fecal material (poop), they carry germs on their feet, which can then spread to whatever else they crawl on.

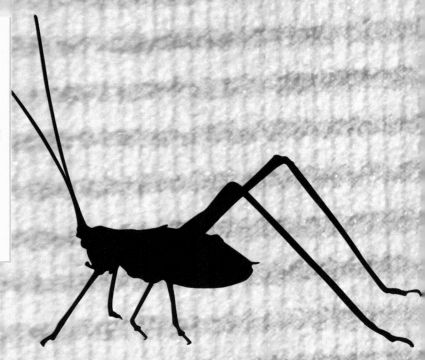

INSECTS THAT SPREAD DISEASE

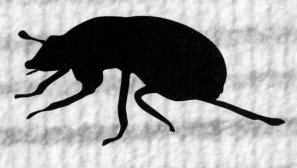

Especially in parts of Africa, Asia, and South America, mosquitoes carry malaria and other diseases. Ticks in North America and Europe spread Lyme disease and other diseases. Other insects can carry other sicknesses. As the Earth's temperature goes up, the numbers of these insects will increase as well—and more people will get sick.

WORDS TO KNOW

Larvae: one of the stages in the life of an insect. When an insect's egg "hatches" the little "worms" that come out are called larvae.

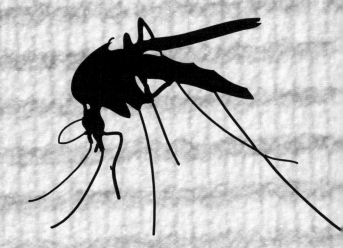

INCREASED AIR POLLUTION

I live in the country. Do I need to worry about air pollution?

A: Air quality is usually better in the country than in urban areas where there are lots of cars and factories. But think about sitting in the No Smoking section of a restaurant or other public place. If someone is smoking, even on the other side of the room, eventually that smoke spreads to the No Smoking section.

The same thing happens with the Earth's air. Pollution doesn't pay any attention to cities' or nations' borders; air pollution spreads through the atmosphere. It doesn't stay put but seeps around the planet. And global warming affects the entire planet's atmosphere, both in the country and in cities. Pollution is the entire Earth's problem.

The "greenhouse effect" that causes the Earth's temperature to rise acts like a lid on a pot—it holds in the air pollution so it can't escape. This means that ozone and other chemicals build up in the air we breathe. This can be dangerous to your health. How dangerous it is depends on who you are and how much ozone is in the air. Most people only have to worry about ozone exposure when ground-level *concentration* reaches high levels. In many cities, this can often happen during the summer months. In general, as ground-level ozone concentrations increase, more and more people will feel sick. More people go in the hospital for breathing problems. People who already have asthma feel worse.

WORDS TO KNOW

Concentration: how much there is of something in another substance. When concentration is high, there's a lot of whatever it is.

Ozone can also make it so you can't breathe in as much air, which means your body has less oxygen. This in turn will change how your entire body feels and how well it works. If you breathe air that has lots of ozone in it for a long time, it can permanently hurt your lungs. People who are very young, very old, or who have breathing problems already are most likely to get sick from breathing lots of ozone. When ozone levels are very high, though, everyone should do what they can to breathe less. This means people should try not to exercise outdoors. They should stay inside as much as possible.

Doctors say that ozone hurts the inside of the lungs in a way that's a lot like getting a bad sunburn on your skin. Ozone hurts the cells that line the lungs' airways. Within a few days, the damaged cells are replaced and the old cells are shed, much in the way that skin peels after a sunburn. If this kind of damage happens many times, the lungs may change permanently. They may become sick or unable to do their job.

DID YOU KNOW?

SMOKE + FOG = SMOG

The word "smog" was first used by Dr. Henry Antoine Des Voeux in 1905 in a paper he wrote called "Fog and Smoke," for a meeting of the Public Health Congress. The 26 July 1905 edition of the London newspaper *Daily Graphic* quoted Des Voeux, "He said it required no science to see that there was something produced in great cities which was not found in the country, and that was smoky fog, or what was known as 'smog.'" The following day the newspaper stated that "Dr. Des Voeux did a public service in coining a new word for the London fog."

DID YOU KNOW?

When the temperature is 130° F (54° C) or higher: *heatstroke/*sunstroke is highly likely.

When the temperature is 105–130° F (40–54° C): sunstroke, *heat cramps*, or *heat exhaustion* are likely if you stay in the heat for very long.

When the temperature is 90–105° F (32–40° C): sunstroke, heat cramps, and heat exhaustion are possible if you stay outside long or exercise in the heat.

When the temperature is 80–90° F (27–32° C): you may feel very tired if you stay in the heat for very long or exercise in the heat.

WORDS TO KNOW

Heatstroke: a life-threatening condition where the body can no longer control its temperature.

Heat cramps: muscle spasms in the legs and stomach caused by high temperatures.

Heat exhaustion: heavy sweating; weakness; cold, clammy skin; a weak pulse; fainting; and vomiting, all caused by spending time in high temperatures.

Global warming not only causes the Earth's average temperature to go up by a few degrees—it is also causing heat waves to happen more often around the globe. During a heat wave, the weather is unusually hot. It usually lasts from a few days to over a week.

Heat waves are dangerous to our health. Heat makes the human body have to work harder than it does normally. This causes stress and weakness. Eventually, it can even cause death.

Older people whose hearts are already tired or sick are most likely to have serious health problems during heat waves. When these people do not have air conditioning or anywhere they can go to get away from the heat, they are most in danger.

On very hot days, try to give your body a break. Don't exercise as much or as hard. Find some place cooler, even if it's only the shade from a tree. Go swimming if you can. Give yourself permission to be lazy. Your body will thank you!

STORMS

DID YOU KNOW?

Hurricanes and typhoons are both given people's names. A name is "retired" once it's been used for an especially strong storm. These names have all been used and won't be used again:

Agnes	Alicia	Allen
Andrew	Anita	Audrey
Betsy	Bob	Camille
Carla	Carmen	Celia
Cesar	Cleo	Connie
David	Diana	Donna
Elena	Fran	George
Gilbert	Gloria	Hortense
Irene	Janet	Joan
Louis	Katrina	Marilyn
Mitch	Opal	Roxanne

WORDS TO KNOW

Typhoons: violent tropical hurricanes/cyclones that occur in the west Pacific Ocean and the Indian Ocean.

In the last few years, people have noticed that there have been more bad hurricanes and *typhoons* than ever before. Scientists think that global warming may be to blame.

Global warming doesn't create hurricanes, but it does make them stronger and more dangerous. Because the ocean is getting warmer, tropical storms pick up more energy and become more powerful. So global warming could turn a smaller storm into a bigger storm. Scientists have found that hurricanes and typhoons have become more dangerous and done more damage over the past thirty-five years.

49

DROUGHT

A drought is a period of months or years when a region doesn't have enough water. Usually this happens when there's not enough rain. When this happens, it can mess up the balance of the ecosystem.

In some regions of the world, droughts have lasted for years and years. When this happens, wildlife dies and farms can't grow food. Sometimes people starve. This is what's been happening in parts of Africa during the past *decades*.

Some droughts only last a few weeks—but even those can damage farmland and wildlife.

Scientists say that every year an area of fertile soil the size of the nation of Ukraine (or the U.S. state of Texas) is lost because of drought.

Drought is a normal climate pattern in some parts of the world—but global warming is making droughts come more often and last longer. In many parts of Africa, people are suffering and sometimes dying because of droughts. Food and water shortages also trigger conflicts and violence.

WORDS TO KNOW

Decades: ten-year periods.

The problem could get even worse. Scientists say that as mountain *glaciers* melt in the Earth's rising temperatures, some of the world's biggest rivers (which are fed by the mountain glaciers) could also disappear. Without these water sources, people will have nowhere to go for water during times of little rainfall. The *rainforest* could die. Without the Earth's millions of trees, our atmosphere will suffer even more.

Global warming is a serious problem. We can't ignore it and hope it goes away. We have to do something! And we have to do it now!

WORDS TO KNOW

Glaciers: slow-moving rivers of ice.

Rainforest: the heavily wooded tropical areas where rainfall is heavy.

DID YOU KNOW?

Drought has many short-term and long-term effects for both humans and nature. It can cause:

- forest fires
- malnutrition
- unemployment
- destruction of wildlife species
- increased poverty
- population migrations (movements) to different places

WHAT SHOULD WE DO?

We need to build cleaner cars and factories that won't pollute our air so much. And we need to use less oil. Instead, we should get our energy from sources that don't damage the environment. Wind, water, sun, and the heat inside the Earth are all clean energy sources that will never run out.

DID YOU KNOW?

If we all changed the way we lived in simple ways, we could help save the environment. For instance, using wind energy is better for the air than burning coal to make electricity. if you eat food that is grown close to where you live, instead of being shipped from across the world, you cut down on the greenhouse gases that would have been put in the atmosphere by the trucks and ships carrying the food. So even the way you eat can make a big difference to our planet!

A Story From Real Life

Africa's Lake Tanganyika, the longest fresh-water lake in the world and the second deepest, gives homes and food to many living creatures. Human beings get fish for food from the lake. Many of Tanganyika's 350 species of fish live nowhere else on Earth. The lake has a ecosystem that's one-of-a-kind: up until recently, its water has been almost all the same temperature, even in its deepest water, 4,700 feet (1,432 meters) down. Unfortunately, global warming may be changing Lake Tanganyika. Even a few degrees difference in temperature kills fish. Millions of people are losing their livelihoods.

Seph, a fisherman on Lake Tanganyika, said that fishing is much more difficult now than it was thirty years ago when he was a teenager. "Oh, it was so good," he said. "When we used to fish with our fathers, it was really good. There were so many dagaa [a type of sardine]. People could fish 5,000 tons. In tons! Back in those days there was so much dagaa."

The people who live on Lake Tanganyika's shore need nature to make a living. Seph said, "We fish because we have no other job. Our grandfathers fished here. Our fathers fished here. We'll fish here and pass it on to our children who will fish and pass it on again. It's our *legacy*."

If the fish disappear, what legacy will Seph—and the fishers of other waters around the world—leave for their children?

WORDS TO KNOW

Legacy: something valuable that is passed down from parents to children.

WHAT IS THE WORLD DOING?

On December 11, 1997, many of the world's nations met in Kyoto, Japan, to talk about what could be done to stop climate change. As of June 2012, about 190 countries are part of the Kyoto *Protocol*. This means they have promised to cut back the greenhouse gas their nations put into the air. The world knows this is a big problem. Scientists, governments, and ordinary people are all getting involved.

Protecting the Earth means we all need to change the way we live. We can no longer use things and throw them away. We can no longer burn gas, oil, and coal to run our cars and factories. We have to find new ways of doing things!

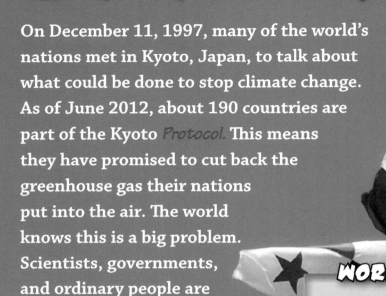

WORDS TO KNOW

Protocol: the terms of a treaty (an agreement between nations).

DID YOU KNOW?

The United States is one of the few nations that has not signed the Kyoto Protocol. And Canada recently stopped following the Protocol.

55

WHAT CAN YOU DO?

Waste is anything thrown away that could hurt the environment. You can keep waste from going into the environment by practicing the three R's of waste management: REDUCE, REUSE, RECYCLE!

REDUCE

Buy and use less! Don't use store bags. Whenever you can, use things that last and can be used many times. Don't use disposable items.

REUSE

Use cloth gift bags instead of wrapping paper or paper gift bags. Use cloth napkins instead of paper napkins. Share outgrown clothes with people who need them—or have a yard sale.

RECYCLE

Don't throw things away—take them to a recycling center instead. Just about anything in your home (or office or school) that cannot be reused CAN be recycled into something else. You'd be amazed what can be done with a recycled product! A recycled soda bottle, for example, can be made into T-shirts, combs, or hundreds of other plastic goods that can be used for many years.

CLEAN AIR

If we want to save our planet—and keep ourselves healthy as well—we all have to do our part. The Earth's health and our own go together! We must all do what we can to protect our air, water, and land.

Here are some things you can do:

Walk or ride your bicycle instead of getting a ride. Plant trees that put oxygen back into the air. Use light bulbs that don't take as much electricity. Turn off lights when you're not using them. Unplug *appliances* not in use.

WORDS TO KNOW

Appliances: the machines in your home, like the refrigerator, the television, and the computer.

EVERY LITTLE BIT HELPS!

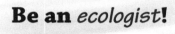

Be an *ecologist!*

Ecologist: a person who studies the relationship of living things to each other and to what's around them.

FIND OUT MORE

National Institute of Environmental Health Sciences
kids.niehs.nih.gov/games/coloring/index.htm

Clean Water
www.ci.oceanside.ca.us/gov/water/clean/default.asp

Environmental Protection Agency (EPA) for Kids: Water Pollution
epa.gov/owow/NPS/kids

European Space Agency (ESA) Kids: Air Pollution
www.esa.int/esaKIDSen/SEM2WKXJD1E_Earth_0.html

Kids 4 Clean Air
www.clean-air-kids.org.uk

National Geographic Kids: Recycling
kids.nationalgeographic.com/kids/stories/spacescience/water-bottle-pollution

Pollution
science.pppst.com/pollution.html

Tiki the Penguin: Pollution
tiki.oneworld.net/pollution/pollution_home.html

PICTURE CREDITS

Harding House/B. Stewart: pp. 48–49
iStockphotos: p. 19, 20, 23, 27, 29, 30, 55, 58
Aswad, Jasmin: p. 46
Babus, Octavian Florentin: p. 43
Boston, Franck: pp. 62–63
Braun, Michael: p. 37
Bryson, Jani: p. 56, 58
Chevrier, Jeff: p. 35
Dammann, Derek: p. 16
de Leseleuc, Julie: p. 42
Delmotte, Gilles: p. 24
Dolenc, Karl: p. 25
Fera, Joy: p. 13
Helbig, Tobias: p. 50
Kaulitzki, Sebastian:
pp 1–4, 17, 21,
Kooi, Paul: p. 34
Leite, Eduardo: p. 55
McCarthy, Martin: p. 47
Meckelmann, S.: p. 11
Newman, Stacey: p. 12
Plougmann, L.E.: p. 54
Stephens, Jacom: p. 32
Tarao, Mayumi: p. 18
Tolmats, Kais: pp. 57–59
Turudu, Emrah: p. 64
Walker, D.: pp. 1–4, 10, 60–61
Zele, Peter: pp. 8–9
Jupiter Images: pp. 12, 13, 14, 15, 22, 26, 27,
28, 31, 36, 38–39, 40–41, 44–45, 52–53
van den Bergh, Frank: p. 54

ABOUT THE AUTHOR

Rae Simons has written many books for young adults and children. After writing this book, she has become convinced that she and her family need to do more to help protect the environment.

ABOUT THE CONSULTANT

Elise DeVore Berlan, MD, MPH, FAAP, is a faculty member of the Division of Adolescent Health at Nationwide Children's Hospital and an Assistant Professor of Clinical Pediatrics at the Ohio State University College of Medicine. She completed her fellowship in adolescent medicine at Children's Hospital Boston and obtained a master's degree in public health at the Harvard School of Public Health. Dr. Berlan completed her residency in pediatrics at the Children's Hospital of Philadelphia, where she also served an additional year as chief resident. She received her medical degree from the University of Iowa College of Medicine.

Made in the USA
Lexington, KY
17 April 2017